THE KNOPF POETRY SERIES

THE MUSE OF DISTANCE

THE MUSE OF DISTANCE

POEMS BY

ALAN WILLIAMSON

ALFRED A. KNOPF

NEW YORK

1988

FOR MY DAUGHTER, ELIZABETH

Library
University of Texas
at San Antonio

THIS IS A BORZOI BOOK
PUBLISHED BY ALFRED A. KNOPF, INC.

Library of Congress Cataloging-in-Publication Data

Williamson, Alan.   The muse of distance.

    I. Title.
PS3573.I45623M87   1988   811'.54   87–45573
ISBN 0–394–56366–2
ISBN 0–394–75577–4 (pbk.)

Manufactured in the United States of America

First Edition

CONTENTS

I V.

ACKNOWLEDGMENTS

Some poems in this work were originally published in the following publications: *Ironwood, The Massachusetts Review, The New Republic, The Paris Review, Pequod, Shenandoah, Sulfur* and *The Yale Review.*

"Recitation for the Dismantling of a Hydrogen Bomb" was originally published in *The American Poetry Review.*
"From An Airplane" was originally published in *The Missouri Review.*
"Robert Lowell: His Life" was originally published in *Ploughshares.*
"The Chair" and "Sandy" were originally published in *Poetry.*

Grateful acknowledgment is made to Farrar, Straus & Giroux, Inc. for permission to reprint excerpts from "Flight To New York" from *The Dolphin* by Robert Lowell. Copyright © 1967, 1968, 1969 by Robert Lowell. Excerpt from "Half a Century Gone" from *Notebook 1967–1968* by Robert Lowell. Copyright © 1973 by Robert Lowell. Reprinted by permission of Farrar, Straus, & Giroux, Inc. Rights in the British Commonwealth excluding Canada administered by Faber and Faber, Ltd.

FALLINGS FROM US, VANISHINGS

Sometimes you came home from the beach with a wasp-sting, or
a speck of sand that even the eye-cup wouldn't wash out.
The day was troublingly larger for being spent
empty, among bodies—as if some great purpose
had been found or missed, looking out to the stationary
water-intake boat, the *crib* (did anyone live there?).
And when you got home, and the sun stayed insidiously
involved in your skin, all indoors seemed delicious
and temporary, like a glass of water.

Or in the early autumn dark, when you came out of
a movie theater, and something cruel, from another world—
the plague; a slave crushed dragging a stone for the Pyramids—
stayed with you, you were afraid to go out to the end
of the long hall, where the small one crooked off to the bathroom,
sensing it, and you, would shelve off into another
space you could feel, though you couldn't know or explain . . .

And it was almost a relief to carry the telescope down
and set its metal legs with a small crisp tinkle
on the playground asphalt (the city stood around silent
like its cardboard skyline in the planetarium).
And then the slight shock of floating out through your eye
to those bodies of gas and nothing, the Coal-Sack Nebula,
across the clean, unlivable, untraversable years.
It made you imagine the world was God's body, split
from some first atom, that was neither world nor God.
You wrote about that for school—"accounts of Creation"—
then refused to read it aloud, because no one else's
was like it, the boys' all science, the girls' all Biblical.
But while you thought about it outdoors, the dangerous night
held its distance; or if not, you could hear it far off, coming
with the same slight ping over the wintry ground.

THE CITY

—A kind of map of the mind, or of life . . .

Eastward, in the fragile curtain we lived in,
all brilliance, tracery, flutings, the mind's feminine
enchantment with itself—crystalline rooms—
it blows against the Lake,

                        light out of darkness,
as the long parks at its feet, abandoned now
to monstrosity, for those hours,
tell you by night; as the gloomy, steeped and over-steeped
last oak leaf of its brick tells you by day.

(One night, a man in one of those towers saw
a shadow detach from the tree-shadow and steal after
a woman, oblivious, in the sulphur brilliance
of the arc lights. She was dead when he put down the phone.)

Then the space behind, with nothing to stop it—beginning
in the loneliness of certain upper
office stories, hundreds of snowy doors,
in the buildings downtown; hurled westward on the El's
black interruption of the air of Gilded
Age shopping streets, to the neighborhoods where life
grew violent and thin with reduplication,
like the great letters stencilled in a fungus
of end-of-winter lavender, char-black, rose,
on the walls where the ads have passed.

Somehow I never felt the invisible country
as ending it (notwithstanding the bits
of green at the moraine rise, distant banners
in summer's heavier, wavy industrial air)—

4

any more than the Lake, with its visible, invisible
far shore, ended anything.

            If there was culmination
near the shales of the beaches, in the blankness
of late November, it was those eyes opening
on endlessness, the museums:
                  out past the small airfield,
spun silk of comets dream-depthless in the slightly
brown far space of early
observatory plates; or the glowing ring
of the Table of the Elements, rounded warily
for fear of the whistle from the reconstructed
coal mine grazing the dome beyond.

                  It was in an under-
ground lecture chamber there, all muralless blank tan
plaster, I heard of *The Birth
and Death of the Sun*; the earth made uninhabitable
in the last explosions.
                  That I and everyone
I knew would be dead, didn't help. My friend thought we would have
    colonized ;
other solar systems by then. I pinned my hopes
on a race of people who had learned to travel
at the speed of the earth's turning, living constantly
westward, on the cusp of the sun's rising,
in a new kind of car that hovered inches
above deserts and oceans; sometimes gaining an hour
or two of night, to sleep in something still
not fire-twisted beyond use; some thing like the Field Museum's
caveman's cave . . .

THE CHAIR

The ten years I've owned it, unapproachable:

Shaker-square; its bottom a cage; its seat
tight-woven, tobacco- and pale-cornhusk-speckly
as an old man's hand, with almost no give from the years
it gave you comfort, the window behind, light falling
from the desk lamp; on the wall, the bitten-in iron wrinkles
of King Charles and John Dryden . . .   It was where you lived,
except for the long planetary loops
through the apartment, your face appearing, eager,
at my reluctantly open adolescent door.

Once a famous man, who revered you,
described your first class of the term. You were having a
     controversy
with another scholar. You came in, laid your green Harvard bookbag
down, took out a book and stared straight into it
until you sensed the students were all
assembled; then looked up and began, "Now *he* says . . ."

Too often, too early, I was the "he" that said
something that could not be swallowed, or let pass.
A thousand miles away, I've had to follow
the endless, cornered turnings of your hurt
reasoning—the chair, the stillness, the long hall—
like a chess partner, unable to withdraw
my attention, because you could not withdraw yours,
day after day, hour after hour . . .
I cannot sit in it to think or write.

Yet how hard you tried to escape from it, the years after
your first illness, when I was twelve—

to enjoy without doing: listening for an hour,
after lunch, to your records of the new, sad, witty
French music, *Les Six*—though really almost preferring
to search out newer ones in the catalogues . . .

Or how we "broke in" our new Ford
each bright fall weekend, driving north
in the white sickle of the autumn light
and your easily angered travel-nerves, to Yerkes
Observatory—prism of leaves downhill
to the cold lake—or the bratwurst restaurant
you remembered, in Milwaukee, from before I was born.

And after, returning, caught on the expressway
in the choke of early dark, moving with the other
accidental cars—the seamed tired faces, children
restless in back, in blue—
                                        I thought of the
empty apartments they moved to scattering leaflike
as their presence beside us in the night, one slipping
ahead, one returned by magic as our lane
slid forward. And back at last, heating our makeshift
meal out of cans, it took a while for the glaze
of home to settle again onto our own
echoing cavern, brown Braques and Légers.

I wanted us so to be happy and at ease,
and we were, halfway; so something clings
about our objects, still crying out
for something more to be done with them, and yet nothing
that is not betokened in the calm and stillness
of their deep shine.

And the chair, where once
I hid in the under-cage and watched the sun
whiten the dust-motes . . .   As I grow older, it seems
to go on getting smaller: when I am dead,
I can imagine it no longer human-
scale, still perfectly polished, in some museum
of styles or souls—strange ones, tied to their places
as a child to his cradle or a martyr to
his tongs . . .

               In their bright shirts, without ties,
the new easy people pass our cage and comment
on the turn of the century; Protestantism; the grimness
of Swedes; the fastidiousness
and guilt of those who rise
above their origins; the long winter of the Great Plains . . .
I am always half gone on with them and half
held back by my need to argue with,
convince, demolish, do justice to and shield
and rescue you—cage and prisoner,
but, while I live, never not the scale of life.

MR. BROWN

He came from a small town in downstate Illinois,
and couldn't believe it when his city students
laughed at the notion that you could hear the corn grow
on soft summer nights. He got me to eat
a fried grasshopper once. His chuckle came low and bland
from inside his sheath of baby fat; his eyelids
were neatly, symmetrically pursed, like the valves of a clam.

Between assurances that our easily sliced-up
flatworm, named Elvis,
would regenerate in days, he was the class
matchmaker. He gave us shyer ones lists of girls
to ask to the Prom; and then—as no adult
had ever spoken to me—"Who knows? You might
give it all up, get married, go and work
in the steel mills. That's the power of your chemistry.
I mean the chemistry of your body, of course."

No date that time. But later, the thought of smokestacks
in South Chicago, across the dreamlike gulf
from the school towers,
helped bridge the other gulf when Karen, dancing,
said in her sensible voice, "Hold me closer,"
as if it were no more than Mr. Brown showing me
a firmer way to shake hands . . .

When the jocks started saying, "Brown's a homo"
in the locker room, I thought with stricken loyalty,
if he is, I must be too; then when he crooked a finger
under my belt buckle, talking in the hall,
a holy dread . . .

                  till tamed by absence, though never listed

matter-of-factly among "gay" friends, he stood,
a kind of Terminus, or excluded Moses, over
the long descent to where we are ropes, ribbons
bird shrill electric outlets dizziness
like the first seawater's, waking to its own presence
somehow jelled from the sun . . .

THE MUSE OF DISTANCE

What composes a life? Mine comes, too much, from books;
but also the sense that, if you climbed high places,

you would see the streets go on with nothing to end them,
and be driven to, perhaps even desire,

whatever they withheld: a flight of smokestacks past water;
a girl in a mean, dawn-blue room; a glimpse of the terrible

engines, or giants, it took to make such a world . . .

*

Far in the caverns of our night, a jarring:
then chinks of light

at both doors to my room, and sausage-smells from our huge
travellers' breakfast; then lugging the suitcases, down

from the hiding-places where they'd kept all winter—
tribal ochre: the trademark an Indian's head

off an old penny—down the long stairwell, black
rail, white balusters, to the mirroring black-

and-white tile at the foot, not scarily dim now, but bathed
through the jewel-faceted panes

of the entrance hall beyond, in silveriness
without origin or ray . . .   So our years came round, as far back

as I can remember, to this ritual of detaching
ourselves from ourselves westward:

our summer in California; half the continent's
breadth; a journey reliving

my father's childhood, failure by fresh start, westward;
which was, perhaps, why his nerves flared to get away

at seven, on schedule, so that he lashed out at
my mother or me, some wrong way I packed the trunk

or failed to make it lock—"If you grew up
the way most people do, that's what your precious

intelligence would be judged by!"—betraying not only
me, but his whole life there, with the quiet,

the high-ranged books . . .   And yet the happiness,
the *Nunc Dimittis*, when we set our course down

the east-west numbered streets, half-fused with the sun risen
from the lake behind us, touching with unwitnessing strangeness

—as, back in the apartment, I had touched
the dinosaur bones on my dresser, knowing nothing

would change their position or how the light would pass them
all the days till fall—the dewy Gothic mirage

of the University; the Negro blocks; the airport's
prairie-tan lanes . . .

When we passed the garbage dump, my father marvelled
in hoots and youks, and held his nose, as if everything

he hated in his life were exposed, concentrated,
rotted and burned at once. For the next half hour—

the country coming on, meadowlarks starting
from the wet ditchgrass, but the great heat rising

more unimpeded than ever in the city—
he sang:

   You were my girl in cal-i-co,
   I was your bashful barefoot beau,
   I wrote on your slate, I love you so,
   When we were— a couple— of kids!

*

My Great-Uncle George hopped the train where it slowed
for the curve near the family farm
eight miles out of Galesburg. He'd done it often,
but this January night couldn't awaken
conductor or passengers. I can imagine
the corridor through the window, lucid, empty,
and how he managed, in the gathering speed, to unbuckle
and reloop his belt around some grip.
                     They found his
frozen body still hanging there in the gaslight
of the Chicago yards.

                I imagine my father
was named for him, whether before or after
I've no idea. In any case, they moved West
so early and repeatedly, the death

could only have followed like a kind of legend
or coat-of-arms.

     Often, crossing the Midwest,
on the new bypass skirting some blind place-name,
my father would say, "I went to high school here,"
or "we had a farm," and then "only my poor father
would have bought such land. I suppose they bailed him
out. They always did."

      We never stopped to visit
those family places, though once we were turned away
at the Brown Palace dining room in Denver, because
I had no tie on. (I was fourteen.)
"Take a look anyway," my father said shyly,
and nudged me past a door—the wrought-iron well
above the lobby, leather sofas: "That's where
I sat and held the gold brick!"
        —a real one;
for maybe half an hour, while Uncle Alvin
went upstairs and made his calls.

Next morning we drove out an indeterminate, elm-lined boulevard
to a lavender-Gothic house. When I got out
to take a picture, he said I was "making a spectacle";
and then, as we pulled away, "it must have been here
that I had the t.b. That bilious attic room."

And I said, "It *must*? But Daddy, don't you know?"

Then off again: but that night I wondered
just what he was revisiting when, as often,
he groaned himself to sleep.

(Though my mother once
returned from the thin-walled motel bathroom, her voice
a mixture of panic and triumph—"They were saying,
*'do you think there's something wrong
with that man in there?'* "
                              —it was not an
unmusical sound: long, falling, half a sigh,
like wind in the wires, or a train distancing.)

                              *

But what I remember best are the anonymous towns
whose Main Streets we walked at twilight, drugged
with the slow lift of six-hundred-mile days
—not even stared at: as though our speed were written
like a protective mark, across our brows—
in those Main Streets still smelling of grass, or the desert's sharpness . . .

It was the things that wrenched at me the most
in those places: a dead firm's name still silver-dollared
in the cool pavement between new display windows;
and all the tools, that lived and toughened and rusted with
men's hands—the unsold harvesters shining
in the first fall light, more terrible than the graveyards
one passed on the outskirts, Indian-fringed with alders . . .

The things were like a song, that could only be heard near the earth,
only two or three inches above it: of men becoming
what they did to live; of raw skill, contempt for the mind;
or just of conditions, equal and without rancor,
of the slow flesh, that has no hope not to vanish
with all it touches . . . whispering, near the earth.

15

And yet if it was high summer, and the road wound
along the bluffs where the tall old scalloped houses
stood embraced by verandas, I invariably
would ask my mother, "Don't you wish we lived here?"
She would sigh, or else be drawn—*of course not, no
theater, no art museums, no real friends*—

And she was right: I didn't, really; what I loved
were the Triple A timetable cards, *Vandalia
16 minutes, 30 minutes Centralia*;
the never quite being in one place, the wind
always the same through the scarcely opened windows;

and yet being everywhere; and, as I grew older, imagining
someone waiting—as if I were called to scatter love
like a wanderer scattering apples, through death's arbitrary
stations and ends . . .

*

*—When the moon moves and the bare driftwood splinters
stand out on the Nevada station wall
I close my eyes, lie on a hard bench, and see
when I am too guilty to picture you, it is you,
the scarps toward your breasts . . .*

—It is last year's antlers, pointing somewhere in the mountains.

*—Yes, you were always one for pointing elsewhere;
and yet there is no place you have not given.
You always lived in the only house with a tower
in the level prairie town.
Your hair was the red Southern clearing, its snakes and lianas;*

16

your eyes a torn screen door
somewhere flashing on coolness.
The empty watery taste of motel air at day's end
is a scarf
you left behind you,
a view of weeds in new earth by a train scar.

And when we meet at the last cottonwood
going into the desert,
drawn up in the dry whisper
of her leaves on themselves
over and over,
will we spring together
into the final jewelcase of the air?

—We are lying together so far across the moonlight,
you can feel the weeds start growing through your hair.

*

Aunt Mary Alice always asked if the girls I liked
had auburn hair. Uncle Harold, she said, always
liked auburn-haired girls—
                            though hers was dark, darker
than the foxfur stole I loved on her, with the real
little teeth and paws, and the little tawny depthless
glass-chip eyes.

                —This was beyond the desert,
beyond the distance where America
almost floats off in the blueness between mesas
and thunderheads, an opaline shudder neither
transparence nor obstruction . . .

                                        beyond that end, a city
that seemed a slightly seasick form of motion,
sea palms and mountain pines, the smell of driving,
the center always just behind you—unless

it centered, as for me, up stairs exhaling
dry stucco, in a room with carefully kept
American coin silver, the mantel clock bonging,
and a sampler with not HOME SWEET HOME but a woolly
locomotive, car, and ocean liner, and OVER
THE LAND / OVER THE SEA / TRAVELLING FAR AND WIDE.

And under it, leg raised and gauzed, no traveller
but a man cars couldn't keep from leaping onto—
off of jacks; unnoticed and unbraked in driveways—
until he had little underarm skin left to be grafted
and "take," or not, over long weeks, on his leg's
reopened tread,
                        my Uncle Harold sat waiting,
eyes bulging as he talked, a rapid-fire
high harmonica twang of hyperbolic
bewilderment, that comes back a tune without words, or the broken
words of old age: how his footsteps cracked in the air
of subzero prairie mornings; how they drove a hundred miles
to pick up everyone, "out to Burbank, the big bands came there—"

A song heard near the earth, only two or three inches above it . . .

And my father listening, almost abashed, only later
shaking his head at how much he'd heard about fishing trips—
yet fond, and almost guilty; and, for all his professorial
moustache, so like his brother, their long skulls
all angles and knobs, and the hair spurting out of them

in short sparky wires—all hardness, but hardness never
at peace with itself: the expression formal, shy,
and ready to break apart in *Jeepers creepers*
haywire whimsy—like a machine some Futurist
was designing, while they walked to school, on the icy Plains.

*

What held him there in L.A.? —the mantel clock bonging
musically, with a long premonitory rasp
on the quarter hour, that, hurrying time, held it
still, unimportant, adrift . . .

                My grandfather,
in the Depression—the last farm gone, the cow
sold, it was said, "so George could go to college"—
failed to see a streetcar as he came home one sunrise
from his last job, night-watchman
at a warehouse, in L.A. . . .

               And all his children
lingered, except my father, already gone; and one
uncle, whom I hardly knew,
retired early, married late, and bought a trailer,
and lived, it seemed, in a kind of roving family
of trailer-couples, linking up near Christmas
in Guadalajara; in the spring, up Oregon way . . .

depthless, to us, as if he'd stepped off in that air
between mesa and cloud.

*

I thought I knew what Uncle Harold did. Then, once, at our place
(our summer place, in Monterey) a wall-outlet failed.

19

I said, "We'll have to get an electrician."
Uncle Harold said, "I am an electrician."

I said, "You're kidding. I thought you—"
                        and suddenly
I didn't quite know what I'd thought. I looked to my father,
but he just looked surprised, and said with an indefinable
hurt in his voice,
                "Of course your Uncle Harold
is an electrician."

Harold worked for Lockheed: the intricate
circuits that held the big jets up in the sky.
But that wasn't the point: my mother and I were outsiders
on any such ground.
                Sometimes, on the trip, he'd compare
his arm with ours, where it rested, freckle-stained
as a gas station floor, on the rim of the open window—
"I can't tan the way you people do, I only burn";
or watching a home movie, after twenty years, would get angry
at the way she was standing, off by herself, in the hallway
of his parents' house.
                And one winter, in Chicago—

"I'm not going to work in the factory, after all,"
I yelled at him.

(I'd gotten a D in Phys. Ed. For two weeks, total silence
on the subject. I conferred with my mother:

"But those aren't his values. He doesn't play ball, or—"

And she: "Whatever men want for themselves, for their sons
they want the other."
"But a professor—"

"Just
because they're professors, they can't stop being men . . ."

—leaving me wondering just what *I* was, included
in this sad, superior, helpless, womanly
understanding . . .)

Now, *going to work in the factory*
hung in the lunch-table air. Then my father saying,
with deadly calm,
"Two of my brothers did."

I rushing in heedless, "But Daddy, you were the exception
in your family. If a professor's kid—"

He managed the worldly, world-weary smile of his prose,
feeling fused with intellect. "Oh, I know,
you're the exception—"

"I didn't say that. What I said was, *you* were—"

Then the voice of the Lord in thunder, drowning me out:

"You're the exception! You're always the exception!"

*

Two of my brothers did: it was his wish
he hated, completed in mine.

                       When Uncle Harold
failed to show up for a family reunion, or awkwardly
we had to shift at the last minute and stay
with one of my aunts—
                 As a child, I didn't notice.
Later, the explanations:

                 "He can't touch a drop now, or—"

"He was the one who went down to the morgue when our father—"

But Aunt Mary Alice, looking down at her own
arthritis-jewelled fingers,
said once, "Harold has fine hands, a surgeon's hands.
He wanted to be a doctor, but the Depression—
and 'the cow was sold for George to go to college'—"

When I told my father, he winced, as if he'd bitten
something sour, then sighed, "Harold wanted to be everything.
He was going to write a great novel, and we'd all
be famous from it. He'd make a million dollars
on the movie—"

He didn't, of course. Like my father, he gave
half his paycheck to keep their parents in their own house,
until the sunrise and the streetcar . . .

He *did his duty*, in that brontosaurian
language my father spoke more, when they'd been together,

as he laughed at jokes on "the colored"; remembered his
    Model T Ford.

*

When "the t.b." returned in him, after years
of late-night writing, slowly angrier nerves,
and he hung in the balance all summer, needing seven
times the normal dose of drugs
                      —small wonder
I turned to Christ, the eternal
son, who dies a little
(or much) to live beyond his father's justice
without calling it a lie.

                    I gave up my childhood anger—
its study of execution and torture, that put the iron
and smoke of Chicago winter into my soul—
in a kind of floating calm, a long June
dusk of forgiveness, in which the city
lay murmuring interfused, the dying
and the newly born.

                    I thought it ungodly to fear death;
though in daydreams I saw my spirit, airborne
above my body, in a hospital bed like my father's,
hover near the bowed heads, ecstatic to tell them how silly
they were not to know how simple it was—then pausing
in a white ceiling corner, not quite sure where to go.

And my father, in his loose-hanging hospital gown,
haggard, slowed down enough to be sweet and wry,
not embarrassed, at my first crush on a girl—

23

making me know the Mystery
was simply true: in suffering, we were reborn.

But, when he recovered, things weren't much changed. He'd still
sing, as on leaving Chicago, the last ten miles
approaching "our shanty." But when we'd actually driven
up Monterey Heights, almost to its scalplock of pines . . .

It's a scene I somehow never entirely escape from.
The fog already coming in; or perhaps not, and glare.
The earthless white granite soil and pine-needle duff.
My parents go over every inch of the house
for "the tenants' " misdoings, every vanished glass or
scratch in the varnish, as if it would tell them what
is missing from what they wanted.

                         Wherever they move, the floor gives
its slight, incurable booming reverberation
from the space too big for a crawl-space and never
finished as a cellar. My father's anger mounts,
shakes everything, ceases, each year, in no particular
proportion to what is lost.

                         I sit in my room, too visible
from the other rooms, the stucco arc of street;
and as I might think of a person—a pair of perfect,
calm, understanding eyes—think of Chicago,
where there are other people, worn gold
interiors to glimpse from the car at night, returning,
in a rush of such black, such deep-gripped-down
cottonwood trees, my own life would grip down
and sleep on itself, dark, full, opening our door
on rich books, peaceful must.

But that is gone
to the far side of the summer. Christ
is less a refuge. If I am not to live
a frozen ghost in the middle wind, a distance
that can never become a place, I must

be here, with them.

*

When I was fourteen I made up a sentence: *we are unhappy
because we have no roots.*
I wasn't sure of it; I'd read something like it in *Time.*
Perhaps we weren't unhappy, or *too many roots*
would have been truer . . .

But I know it struck on
something in me; some place where I was dreaming,
against us, an image of the true house, solid
on the solid land: the summers falling stationary
through the bay windows; piano music dampered
at night, in the thick leaves; and up the stairs
unnumbered branching alcoves, sisters, silences—

like a house in a book, where a distant lake was visible
from one upper window—enough endlessness
to rest a family in each other and
the ground beneath,
                so that, if one lived there, a life
would fall like an image: first love to white stone a falling
of original leaves . . .
                and the unseen sister upstairs
comes out and gathers it all into her hands.

That was my dream, as we passed the small towns sleeping . . .
But what my father remembered (though he could never approve
    of himself
for having arrived there) were the intimations
of a world beyond: how a store would have, from some wanderer,
almost postage-stamp-sized books, *The Ballad of Reading Gaol* or
Non Sum Qualis Eram Bonae Sub Regno Cynarae . . .

And though I said *we are unhappy, we have no roots*, I know
when I reach back as far as I can for an image
of happiness, I come to images of travel:

the DIP signs in the desert, the runningboards
and buck-tan interiors of '40s cars;
or asking my parents, in Needles, California,
one night when I was four, "How far away are the stars?"—

expecting I don't know what, a few city blocks
or even as far as L.A.—and then the vastness
of the answer somehow soothing, as our departure
soothed, back in Chicago, the dinosaur bones, the chairs . . .

We seem contented in vastness, as we do not, wholly,
anyplace solid, where our weight and distance
can be determined . . . in this, "the exception"
though we are forever, most purely American.

OBSESSION

(AFTER RODIN)

Buried, unformed: the head down in the knee's
undented space, as if it too were skin
merely, to prickle at hot and cold, not measure
any shape beyond it. All that has detail is what
is left unfinished: the quarry-rock of hair
that, over the blank spheroid, makes the cup
of an acorn, down to the slight, vestigial stem . . .
It is the thought that has held her so many months
gelled, opaque, unspeakable; to wait
in blind hope that soon—
leaving scarcely a mark, in the twinkling of an eye—
it will slip from the peculiar, perfect egg, and all
that was inside will be spelled out, root into leaf.

SANDY

(V I R G I N I A ;   1 9 7 0 s)

1

At first it's enough just to carry the little gun
to the supermarket—first in one pocket, then
in another. He enjoys the anxiety
of checking for bulges in the shoplifters' mirror.
It gives the aisles an expectancy, a glisten.
He finds he loses his hatred of the women—
the old ones stalled for an hour
in front of a bank of cans, the slightly younger
mowing you down with their carts and pirate smiles.
He learns to allow his eyes to stare.

Strangely, he finds it is often the young mothers
who go most nearly nude there,
bare-bellied under flimsy halters
as the babies who reach up . . .
He is astonished that they can get so angry, and scream so,
way out on the calm white beaches of themselves.

2

He has always wanted to do it in strange
half-abandoned public places: say, a storefront
at midnight, among mannequins, a far spotlight sliding
its sad old-rose refrain across the plaster . . .
Or this: one Sunday, he finds an abandoned quarry
on a dirt road under the mountains,
cliffs of pale dust and sun; a ring of pines.

There is a worn wooden chute in it, leading up
to a kind of house, on stilts,
machinery shadowed through the sieve-like siding.
He would like to climb there, but the underpinnings

go crazy at his weight.

He jumps free in terror, then
goes back to test with his hand; and suddenly
feels his skin cling to the dead silvery surface
in which there is something perfect, something that gives joy
in whorls and waves and does not know what it has
to be joyful about: a transparent house, full of pulleys.

3

At last it is only a question of: this day,
or the next, the next? He stands on the softening asphalt,
hoping the eyes of the colored cart-boy pass
over him easily. Does he choose
by ugliness or beauty: the mocking smile held too long
with no one around to mock, or the glassy sheen
of a summer day on an olive collarbone?

He is at the car window, has shown
the gun; it is over. In a different world
he makes her point the car at the wavering mountains.
She will have to undress in the center, so the light
and dust off the cliffs will glitter on her wholly,
as if a small lake appeared there, to dive in . . .
He has almost forgotten the gun; he dandles
it and vague memories of a magician's wand
across his lap.

He says, "My friends call me Sandy."

IN THE MILITARY MUSEUM

(HÔTEL DES INVALIDES)

I came on you around the corners of the glass armor-
filled cases: bright matte cuirasses with men
chasing shepherdesses, flag-wound crucifixions . . .
And the dust of unplanted courtyards: it hung on everything
unglassed there, but most of all on the worn purple
checks of your sport coat; and your head stooped forward, listening
so intently—for what?—in that forest of shadows of men.

And then the other, his stronger body narrower
in essence;
                    more knitted in space, intensely blond;
looking as if it might step off a hundred miles
at a flicker; as if all it owned were still
invisibly there, on its shoulder . . .

. . . "It's a good place to think about man,
at Bamian. Everyone went through there, Tamburlaine,
Alexander—east, west; and behind you, Phidian Buddhas
a hundred feet high, still dreaming
inside the cave of the rock—"
                                        And his hand
moved, with furtive attentiveness, to touch your shoulder.

"But, Robbie . . ." You flinched back a bit, yet wanted so
to knit your face, the way this face was knit
to yours . . .
                    I stood there spellbound; and after, without following,
I kept meeting—banner, window-embrasure, stair—
the argument of your steps, as if they were my own
in another summer:

                              if the light in your room did not hang
so tiny on its string; if the days planned hour by hour

did not lie, in the end, like graph paper
under the sights seen; if the girls didn't have *un truc*
so hard in their voices; if Robbie's skin
were not so hairless and magnesium-flare
brilliant, like armor . . .

                    perhaps you would not
be following this line of steps out, through
a new city: Algerian pocket-slum to how
to like Poussin, to this . . .   And always walking, Robbie saying
"It's good to measure things against your body."

Paused, now, before the *Black Book* of Nazi tortures.

. . . And if, perhaps, you were not always
half-wanting to outstrip the letters waiting
from a father who often treated you
as if this fate were already upon you . . .
saying, when you got home late, after quarrelling
with your best friend, at eleven, "If he's so wonderful,
why don't you just go home with him and stay there?"
Saying, when you wanted to give up
your part-time job at college, "Such love of oneself
as an end in oneself led to Nietzsche, and Hitler."

His face: that stubbly, alien landscape gradually
taking over your own, just slowly
enough to establish you are unworthy
and cannot escape.

                But what is lost if manhood
is sacrificed to manhood? The earliest, most disinterested, moving
not on comparisons, but expanding spaces . . .

Surely nothing but the words of men
moving on contempt mainly, half-hating their bodies, afraid
to prize too much the only thing they prize.

                                   And now
it is as if these interlocking courtyards, cannon,
indistinguishable stars and boulevards were repeating
the discovery in an empty bedroom that nothing
beyond you is needed: the surface grows brilliant, ratified
by the nerves alone,
as the heroes, perhaps, ratified themselves moving
on the empty desert . . .
                      So to hold one person free
above all the ugly, self-distrusting words
becomes the final, because the most isolating, courage.

I lose sight of you going down into that dreadful
basement
                 where the angel-muses of his victories seem
to hold, with the terrible intentness of their frowns,
the body, which otherwise surely
would never stop sinking in its triple skin
of metals . . .

I feel your sinking, as you round the bend
where so many copies of his raw immortal
torso flash on you, giving laws;
                         yet know
subtly, outside myself,
how the fine gentle nerves of the hand tapping
your shoulder will see you home.

The boys who would never admit they miss their mothers
hate the dietician. When she walks past the tables, at night,
The food eats shit—The food eats shit—they sing—
Hi-ho the dairy-oh the food eats shit. God,
there's little to be proud of there; except that one was not, in
    one's turmoil,
quite as blind as Bernie, who changed his name to B. Dov,

allowing the dining-hall announcer to read, "Beat-off
Lederberg will show his films *Moth-err*
and *Hand-Heat*"—spoon banging, turmoil,
and Bernie: "Read it right, asshole"—"in the Common Room tonight."
And all that freshman talk about sex and God,
the machines we were caught in!—while the late-night hissing

of the radiators gave way to the long singing sweep of wind up our hill; or rain, far off.
"We are being pissed on from the prick of God,"
my roommate said. And I thought how they—the fathers and mothers—
wouldn't understand, not seeing how cosmic Night
loomed on us, and the gallantry of our turmoil.

I don't feel any easier now about that turmoil,
or surer what part of it still sings.
Nothing rubs the deeper blackness from those nights.
It was one thing to talk all the time about "beating off,"
another to push a door, not meant to give, and (*mother-
fucking lock!*) a friend's hand, nailed to its terrible god.

I thought my Christian friend was looking for God,
when he walked out into the snowstorm, that spoke to his turmoil,

like Oedipus vanishing into the gorge of the Mothers.
But what tormented him was another singing,
and the whiteness so electric—he couldn't just beat off—
but had to walk, imagine glances, risk knives, all the city's night.

Was that the night I realized how our night
was full of music, like an island full of gods?
Only say that you'll be mine—someone's banjo off
somewhere—*And in our home*—*happy*—that turmoil—
Down beside where the waters flow—and mix and sing
(in whose room, on what floor?) the future, the murder, the mother.

It seems a kind of off-key voice of God,
that singing always somewhere, under the night,
motherly, lonely; repeating and changing our turmoil.

ART ROMAN

(AUTUN, DECEMBER;
POITOU-CHARENTE, JULY)

The angel wakes us to the star an inch
beyond our heads,
where we sleep, even if we are kings, all under
one cloak . . .

As from the Roman wish to close a gate
on the forest night, *oppidum*

      —we skidded down
the ice-slick hill to see unearthly, shouldering
up from three-story houses—

there comes the arch and weightiness of God:

so from God this endless

      actionless itch to know
ourselves more real?—where we go, half-bent, under
the wind from inside the atom . . .

      and still
they hang a boar by the heels, for the year's turning,
in the butcher's doorway.

      And, over us, the saved,
come from the year's charmed round
of stars and labors, stand
still, with a child's small smile and even locks
for the wind to lift like hay;
and climb like children through the complicated
frail balconies, needing
a boost to the buttocks from the angel standing
below—

      while, opposite, the damned
discover everywhere mouths: a devil howling
to find his hand has clubbed into a crab . . .

But what does God see? This rictus facing nothing
in the scene that ends all things . . .

                               Only
the cancelling-out of justice? Dante would say
He looks into Himself and there sees everything,
as everything, when it looks in love, sees Him—

a dance on a pinhead!

                    —though west and south,
in summer, toward the Cathar kingdoms,
everything divides, everything swallows everything
and lives inside it: the dancer's two
swivelling bodies meet in one head; the lion's
tail is also, seen closely, the crying woman's
arm . . .

                    and for an hour
one believes Dante, in the too tall grass.

THE PRAYER OF THE CATHARS

As little known of them as whether they
actually shared their wives, or on the contrary
prescribed deer-hunting to those incapable
of absolute continence, holding it
a lesser gash in the eternal body . . .

> *For the sake of the good He gives*
> *life to the evil, and will do so*
> *as long as there are any of my little ones in the world*

It is known they could live with Jews, Moslems,
and even Christians; that where the four
touched, the Kabbalah,
the cult of Mary, and Western poetry
sprang up in a hundred years.

For whatever endless reasons
they displeased the world; an army moved south
as we've seen armies move—the jeep's
radio antenna lowered playfully
to catch the old man bicycling downhill
at just the right height and snap
his neck.
          The propagandists, as always,
spoke of it not as something
anyone did by will, but fire
from heaven, the eagle of Zeus, *Anangke*.

> *And the devil was very false,*
> *for he said that God deceived them*
> *in allowing them to do Good only;*
> *and that he would give them wives they would love greatly;*
> *and he gave them commandment over one another,*

so that some should be kings, emperors, and counts,
and that with one bird they might catch another bird,
with one beast, another beast.

If you were a nobleman you had the right
to be beheaded. But they
could choose to cut your arms and legs off
first.
          Commoners, of course, went to the fire.

                    *

    Can vei la lauzeta mover . . .

The song begins: the countertenor voice
rising for the moment when
the sun's first ray transfixes it, and joy
gone to the heart it falls, forgets itself—
forgets, the voice says, its own sex, even the earth—
as, it may be, the Perfect forgot
when they filed down from solar Montségur to die . . .

For the Lady, too, is a mirror from before Nature
looking on whom the self finds the deep sigh
that kills it: lost *com perdet se*
lo bels Narcisus en la fon.

White walls with stammering saints, turned to white bodies.
Nothing survives; or everything
in the shape of its opposite. Their burnt page left
a curve, a bottomlessness
in Europe's certainties—

                    even
the navel and winding Salome's veil of Isaiah's
dance at Souillac—
though for two hundred years the churches
were built with arrow-slits at the crenellations.

    And so they rose upon a heaven of glass,
    and as many as elevated themselves there,
    so many fell and perished;
    but God descended with 12 apostles
    and darkened himself in St. Mary.

PARIS, THE SHORTENING DAYS

What is it asking? The blooming of ironwork roses,
of observatories at the ends of the avenues;

the body still shot through with triangles, trapeze swung
forward, in the medical bookstores;

or winter come with the underwater heaviness
of its distances, a blue shift in the spectrum . . .

No church is endurable in that light but those
too late for the full faith,

where space has forgotten to point itself, expands
in booming, echoing sub-porticoes;

where Samson must flex his thick arms to brace
the pulpit, and the hour hand at noon

go into the lion's mouth.

How the human face always emerges crying
from the rich wood, the stone! —

as if trying to wrench itself free: the same face that
will go on streaming, wild hair out behind,

into the last century, comet on a shop sign;
into this one, live and whitened, in the bars . . .

And a voice left behind in my head, too faded-sounding
to be of use at my work-table, saying

What are the things the spirit falls through to rest?
Water, and well-worked stone, and the faces of women.

TIMES AT CASSIS

On your longest walk you saw the coast's down-slant
three times repeated: in the eaten-under limestone
across the channel; the color of hidden candlelight
under the château, *des Lombards*; then red in the huge cape—
each layer as if wanting to slip undersea, and then
another above, the pressure, and the last
exploding in a little leap of topsoil, pines . . .

And then another uncrinkling
of coastline: the small white mosque of the weather-
station, the *Sémaphore.*

                And you, picking yourself forward,
so lonely, so careful, in the great glare—what
did you have yourself think of? Of the Albigeois,
that page burnt blank, where Europe
almost turned Buddhist, then hinged over
to what seemed the opposite, *Donna
mi priegha;*
            of La Ciotat,
its old town smaller than the tanker *Fazi*
it lives by building;
                or
what you expected from these wanderings, going
ever deeper . . .

            Dissatisfied with yourself when the poetry
of a girl like a figurehead
interposes at a far pine: too long
imagined sex has screened for you
the day—
           its netted, receding swelling; the Sunday sails.

*

Days, days. And yet never as then—childlike,
abandoned to yourself—were they so real to you,
the serene empire of the day that passes,
casting out, drawing in its sails . . . When friends came,
and you could show them the places, you felt
so much more solid it was an emptiness.
Look, you'd want to say, *there's the rock I sit on, the water*
that dazzles under me—as if just to have endured them
with nothing known to sustain you, set you there
forever, a diamond's-end of radiance, empty
focus without bounds . . .

                         some thing like the sudden island
that sprang on you, that day, from behind the rocks—
white lines too inward-torquing for a goat's foot
to stand still on; and seeming
in the late light
to hang, like a ghost-ship,
one royal-purple inch above the waves . . .

And later, after the ghostly walk home—the city
of shut summer villas, their patio trees slowly
straying from a perfect sphere—

                         in the quickened falling
toward sleep, it sometimes seemed to you your head
was the Great Head; the near shore
your hand that kept wanting to pull it back by the hair.

AIRPORTS

Surely someone, finding them, in whatever rubble,
will say someday, these were the greatest temples:
at the ends of the cities, the eye-stalk tower; and then
the parabolas of glass, the fresh-shined floors, that lift us
as if in a chalice to sea-space and blue,
to the endless light of the speeded, upper heaven—

turning places to mirages because we get there through nothing
we could inhabit, no time on our watches; come back
to the same temple elsewhere, the same small jig lightly playing . . .

And yet, from the ground, the obscure comfort of
that incoming map over cities: the sound descending
over and over the same celestial staircase . . .
And the girls in their deep-sky cobalt—no wonder we thought them
so available, yet awesome—the incalculable
quotient of air and death sifting their thighs . . .

*

But when, instead of DELAY, the machine says ASK
beside the flight number; when the relatives, shunted
to a sealed cocktail lounge, complain, "We've had
four ministers and no facts," to the reporters;
while, on the mountain, crews are already summoned
to pick the few still
whole people, with their still just-startled look,
out of the scarred brown trees—

But what has that mountain, calm again in an hour,
to do with these or their waiting? What can anyone understand—
in this labyrinth of ramps, voices out of walls—except
that whatever it is that calls people back from the heavens
does not call theirs; and goes on not calling.

47

THE LIGHT'S READING

(MEDITATIONS ON
EDWARD HOPPER)

1

On Sundays, from upstairs, a grown man's voice:
"I love it I love it I love it I love it Yay
Patriots!"
               What do they love? Or the women's spooky
enjoyment of pity: "Isn't that the way . . ."

A man's voice falling, in a hotel corridor, "Yes,
dear, I'm going . . ."

                    Everywhere we fail
to snatch it back off the mirror, this endless falling
of life that only
lives to keep itself going: impenetrable scrim . . .

2

The light's reading of us: by definition, ending
where it begins, like a clockface . . . at times
endlessly fertile and opening—the sun
presses the girl's crisp summer dress back like wind
where she waits at the hot curb,
and you feel behind her every hoarded coolness
of the dim apartments.

                    But always, come August,
the shadows are folded away; then something happens
in the color of the sky, like a trumpet, calling
to the bronze in things: the leaves, the purple horsetails
of the marshgrass, the crazy shingled houses.

Then the fattish girl comes out in her bikini
to sun, once more, on the rail of the upstairs porch,
her mother knitting behind . . .

It is all in her silly, hopeful look out against
where the painting looks: evening blue
distilled in the roofs; the empty room behind her,
where the sun's rim only reaches the white border
of the picture on the wall; and all the mother is keeping
herself from saying . . .

                  the light, like a reader, in love with fate.

3

The man sleeps, his back a shell. The woman, able to bear more—
if only to bear how much they have desired
each wide-pored, graying other—

                  is sitting up.

He seems to float among monoliths: the walls
thickened with what—mere dusk, a hidden airshaft,
closets, plumbing?—

One sees past every wall to another window.

Inexplicable fear of falling: the ringed horizon,
the eternal smokestacks—

So desire towers, and, towering, holds us
over what is beyond any
object: the empty clockface, the rims of time.

4

A man who loves only one woman in his life
empties the space around him with rejected
dreams.
        It is the shock of their going opens

the air as far as death. The people there
look strange, in that long light: at first, more rigid
than the damned in hell; then the rays find a richness
of old metal in the wrinkles, a smile in the sag of the breast—
shimmer of the impenetrable, the pure cells . . .

Was this love, or simply knowledge of the planet
of his cropped head, what life it would bear?—that kept
the picture from filling
with young girls or children, only these two
comedians, the pancake stiff on their faces,
the smiles stiffly waiting to say good-bye . . .

Yet how delicately he paints her vanishing
to him, at the moment when she stands most lovably
still before life. The sky
is behind her wholly. The frame does not let one follow
her arm even as far as the flex to move
her paintbrush. Her look is gone
into whatever has caught it, leaving only
a sidelong spill of light off the lens of the eye.

FROM AN AIRPLANE

From an airplane the two valley towns seem equal
to each other, along the axis of the mountains,
though the only road between snakes twenty—thirty?—
miles to the north, where narrowing canyons open
the possibility.
                You hold the two
in your eye as in God's hand, the same statistical
print-out of roofs, gone blank with snow; and think
how if you lived there you would love, hate, marry
someone in the next five houses; perhaps never
get as far as the mirror-town, before you died;
or if you started to walk there, how measuredly the cold
would rise in your boots with the first, the second field.

Where you'll land, it's just less visible. In the many
streets and cubicles, someone, just separated,
feels the dead years in his furniture as a measure
like cold in his bootsoles; or he turns back, stays married,
and the unlived town stays in the empty balance . . .
But the restaurants hide it more, the headlines, the friends.

On the whole you'd rather be up here forever,
where the fact that the earth curves is actually visible,
blued with its unexperienceable other time;
not come down at all—unless, of course, you could live
like the Acoma people, stunned for centuries
with the sense of being at the center.
                                    It could absorb
anything, even the Cross: they carried beams
thirty miles on their shoulders from Taylor Mountain,
and any that touched the ground couldn't be used
in the church roof; they were tapered

to candy-cane-colored "candles" for the reredos.
The bells are male and female, because four boys
and four girls were traded to Mexico City for them.
In the pottery, one is always at the center
of interlocking weather—sweeps and stairways
of black, with the little triangles inside them
meaning lightning. It's one of
the thinnest potteries in the world. The ingredients
come from the four directions: north for blackness,
south for white slip, east for yellow slip, west for clay.

THE PUBLICATION OF HISTORY

I once went an hour early to your skyscraper classroom. There,
my fear of death seemed grand and bearable; your large head
was all thought, hung, almost exploding, over emptiness,
as your voice hung, over the cold fire of brick
steeples catching the late light, among concrete hills,
Landor's *Soon shall Oblivion's deepening veil*
Hide all the peopled hills you see . . .
Your head has blown up since then, and dusted the world,
and my fears, too, come back in chalky fragments.
Your book is the sadness of grade-school afternoons
squared off in the same hard-blue and dust-red, the blood
sinking into the plains of our long journey;
and the sadness of checking the locks on all the windows
at night, seeing the ghost of a plant peer through.

THE DRAWER OF PHOTOGRAPHS

We will not find you by going back to London,
not even in another
heat-wave of the century, the fire-alarms ringing
peacefully in the empty buildings all day Sunday . . .

or the floor-through room above Earl's Court, already
otherworldly: two or three chairs; worm-eaten dark
scrollwork around the Jacobean mirror;

the one chest with a thousand snapshots drifted
inches-deep in the drawer—where, at a question, how
a house looked, a friend, your hand went hovering, looking—

*

Yet I cannot help imagining death
as one of your triumphs—down from the high air
where what you loved and feared stood: life
drawn up beside you,
                    Dante
equal in height to Purgatory, *the maker*
can't lift his painted hand to stop the crash

—for you wrote your fate, like many great men, unknowing—

With us no husband could sit out the marriage . . .
But you hung between two, and between two continents, never
quite having to choose—the triumph—arriving dead
at your last true, though still divorced, wife's door;

without a reckoning; almost outside destiny . . .

What shall I do with my stormy life blown towards evening?

—Yet did not die in the air, but touched the earth
an instant—half a lifetime's goal—desiring
to do what others did, without afterthought; the senseless
detail: walked to the taxi line, with your bags;
spoke to the driver, something
weightless about the weather;
slept; weren't there—

*

And the photographs you loved unmounted
at sea in the drawer of your only chest.

EAST ARLINGTON

I stopped there, ten years back, to check a tire,
heading South and home. It stayed with me—an evil
stretch of road, hemmed in by cyclone fences
and cinder shoulders, the town below and hidden
to one side, the other side industrial marshes.
No mechanic on hand. They added air. Behind time,
I didn't care to think the tire might blow
hours later and send three cars balleting
across the Connecticut Turnpike, with, miraculously,
no injuries.
             Or to think my life could grow
so accident-thrown that for two years I'd live there,
on a street of shingle and shadowless-siding houses,
so uniform, one spotted the odd half-window
at an upper landing, in time, as eagerly
as an angel hidden, for God's eyes alone,
in a French cathedral.

But there was a field behind the houses,
an urban field, part marshland in most seasons.
It curved up like the earth to get away from
its horizon of disused tracks and sickly willows,
and the clouds raced across it like the ghosts of the trains.
The city let anyone who wanted to have
an allotment there. Ours was out on the end
and had to be reclaimed, it seemed a foot an hour,
from a turf all roots, bricks, nails, and real New England
granite shards. But it grew beautiful
enough for the twist-mouthed corner toughs to want to
scream through at midnight, at the end of summer,
bending the Portuguese family's iron fences
to curlicues, pulling even the stubborn

eggplants up by the roots.
                              We discovered it at twilight
the following day. All the Sunday gardeners
were standing about; I met a colleague, another
temporary lecturer, I'd always assumed was
some well-off plumber, or office manager.
The police said they knew who'd done it but couldn't move
without an eye-witness.
                        Though my wife and I
had quarreled that day, she said
she couldn't believe my courage when I tamped
the few only-half-uprooted flowers back in,
feeling as I did so how cold the earth
had already gotten, the first killing frost
waiting inches under. But I felt no courage:
a grim, childish tenderness; the one way I had
of mocking evil, or placing my hope in hope.

CONTINUING CITY

"the children no one prays for"—Tomas Tranströmer

For the second time in a year, our boxes gaping
everywhere, then piled up mightily, having eaten
the rooms. I hear you through the wall, put down
for your nap, in the one room left intact,
say to your mother, "I don't want to die";
and remember the desolateness of our first morning
here, how you and I snapped awake at seven
while she slept past ten, blocking
it out; and the house painter let himself in, not knowing.
And so we went out to circle our yard with its strange
earth, bare and lined, as if swept out with a broom,
and named the strange new trees: eucalyptus, orange,
St. John's breadfruit, loquat . . . *Stars of the Land of Pain.*
And the earth steadied a little, as if we'd leaned on it
and it pushed back, saying, like a stewardess,
"We have just landed . . ."

                              Now that bodiliness
scarcely assumed, withdraws. I listen to Anne's voice saying
how we live on in each other; how "things alive
and quick and complex, the way we are, can't be made of
things that last, like metal or stone." You say, "I'd like to
be made of a stone." And I see you for a moment a wondrous
metallic child, each eyelash heavy as prayer
once made us, saying we deserved to live forever.

My anger is pointless; I don't believe it either.
And yet (as all day you go on, insistent
and insupportable, since obsessions
are sincere and still a way of saying

stop the world for me) I keep asking what I could tell you
different, when at last, my turn, I sit
on your bed in the dusk—pale light on California sheetrock . . .

Gods. How they pulled the sun out of the ocean's
wetness. How they receded
as we knew more—but we never quite knew everything . . .
"What does God look like?" "Maybe a little like everything,
since he made everything—"
                              "I think God looks all *grinty*."
You squinch your eyes. "If he knocked on the roof, I'd hide."
Aren't I scared of God, even a little? Did anyone
ever see him? "Well, they saw him
the way you sometimes see something in a dream
and aren't sure you're dreaming . . ." "Then did they wake up?"
"They didn't think so." "But what did he *look* like?"
"Well, *dif*ferent, to different people—" But wanting to give you
some sweetness I felt in our uncertainty
without false hope, I tell you how a man
saw three big circles, different colors, in the sky,
then a beautiful human face; then the two changing
back and forth (he couldn't tell how) into each other.

*

Six months in a new house, the Berkeley winter
crystalline with ocean-light, you tell me, "Sometimes
I don't want to die"; then, "will the world ever die?"
Eliding the bomb, I tell you that maybe billions
and billions of years from now, the sun will explode

and then go out. You're most concerned for the houses.
"I want the houses still to be beautiful for the angels,
when we're all dead."

    And I: "Maybe another world
will start up, when this one ends."

      And you: "Maybe the pretend
animals here will be real ones there,
the zazas and zuzus. I'd like to be a zazu."

RECITATION FOR THE DISMANTLING
OF A HYDROGEN BOMB

From under the flat surface of the planet,
where we know, by statistics, you are waiting,
the White Trains sliding you through our emptiest spaces,
the small grassy doors to you trimly
sunk in the earth by desert or cornfield; then
the neat metal sheath, smaller than a mineshaft, with no
feeling of depth—
            O how will you ever clearly
come to our sight? Surely our mortal hands
must take you, carry you, do, step by step, the terrible
laying you to sleep, or else— There is no third way.

We have seen you, as in the mirror of a shield,
suddenly standing tall on so many sides of us
like beautiful ghosts—able to hold completely
still on your columns of smoke, then making
a slight lateral tilt to take direction.
And then we realized—everything standing, the rattled
watch on the table a-tick—we were the ghosts,
and you, your power, our inheritors.

And turning from the shield, we saw the world
glare back, withholding; as if a nothingness
already lived in bird and twig, and they
turned their backs on us, to know it.
                   But our minds
weren't ready yet; they could only wish and wish you
out of this world, out of ourselves.

   We might have thought of sending you
to wander, like a belled goat, the outer space
our fantasies wander so much now, caged

63

before the dreaming blips of our screens, inventing—
so we are told—a freedom untouched by you.
We would feel the endlessness you were shot into,
in which, if you destroyed,
past the range of our lenses, objects past our knowing,
it would come almost as a lightness, like the sense
of falling that comes before the fall of sleep.
It frees us without cheating you.

                                 For we
are grieved to give up a power—as if time
began to run backwards, our bodies shrank and dwindled
until they reached our mothers' wombs, and disappeared.
Some days we'd even rather
use you, and use you up, than live the centuries
you won't quite vanish—the knowledge leaching through us
like your cores buried, after long debate,
in moon-polished canyonlands, always
a mile or so too near a major river . . .

The stars won't hide you. But there are precedents—
if analogy serves still—places
where things too big for us have been sung to sleep
once we knew we couldn't, or no longer wished to,
kill them.

            The flesh of death lay on the altar;
—or a class where doctors (the one who speaks a woman,
soft-voiced) teach those in permanent pain to focus
on one word, and cross their legs in the right way,
as if singing, silently, to the thing in themselves . . .

My Lord, good night.

So we set ourselves with sorrow down, to sing to you,
sing you from underground. First, of course, come
the treaties, the surveillance satellite cameras
pinpricking the globe—surface anesthesia
for our tireless fear of each other.

                      Then
it is like taking up hands
against some larger shape of ourselves—the skull-like shield,
the outer fissionable cortex, the inner
strange sky of the lighter-than-air . . . The self-destruct
systems (and the circuits that spoke to them, under the mountains) ;
the temperatures, equalled only
"in transient phenomena like exploding
supernovae."

        My Lord, good night

                  —our arm
clad with the sun.

Go to sleep in us, as once, they say,
God went to sleep, and we trembled, not only that nothing
any longer overarched us, but that we
must contain what had.

          (The class is quiet. The doctors
come and go unnoticed, on their beeping

emergency calls. We have gone so far into
what hurts us, whether incalculable nervous twitch
or cancer. Time drifts outside us. Then the voice
—Look at something. Anything. Our eyes open wider
than seemed possible, through blear hospital panes, on things
a little different for each. Brown canyons
of bark. Light combed out past them. End of winter.)

"*Art Roman*"—the French term for what we call "Romanesque"—
means, literally, "Roman art." Moving from the Roman gate at Autun
(which was, in fact, an *oppidum*, a frontier garrison-town) to the
rounded arches of the cathedral, one can see why. The images at the
end of the poem come from Chauvigny, near Poitiers. The art of
Poitou-Charente (not, in fact, a "Cathar kingdom," but nearer to their
part of France) has a metamorphic quality that contrasts sharply with
the beauty and terror—the childlike men, the almost Pre-Raphaelite
women, the tremendous Last Judgments—of the Burgundian churches.

"The Prayer of the Cathars." All of the inset quotations in English
come from a prayer or, more accurately, a credo of the Cathars,
preserved in the records of the Inquisition, which I came across in
France in a book of troubadour poetry (unfortunately, I have lost the
reference). *Can vei la lauzeta mover* ("When I saw the skylark move")
by Bernart de Ventadorn is one of the most famous troubadour love
poems. It is sung by Russell Oberlin on the record "Troubadour
and Trouvère Songs" (*Expériences Anonymes*). I am indebted to many
sources for this poem, but especially to Zoe Oldenbourg's remarkable
and painful novel *Destiny of Fire*, and to Hugh Kenner's *The Pound Era*.

"Paris, the Shortening Days." The churches "too late for the full faith"
are St. Sulpice, St. Etienne du Mont, and St. Merri. The "comet"-like
faces on shop signs can be seen at the Musée Carnavalet. The cadence,
and probably the ambiguous mood, of the last two lines were suggested to
me by the line Aschenbach meditates on in *Death in Venice*: *Oft
veränderten Schmuck und warme Bäder und Ruhe.*

"Times at Cassis." "That page burnt blank": the Church not only
burned the Cathars themselves but destroyed almost all records of their
beliefs and ceremonies, so that heresy would perish forever. Ezra
Pound, and a number of scholars, have believed that the troubadour
cult of the lady was a kind of metamorphosis of a Cathar cult of light.

Donna mi priegha ("A lady asks me") is the first line of Guido Cavalcanti's metaphysical canzone on courtly love.

"The Light's Reading." I have deliberately tried to make the boundaries between "meditation" and descriptions of paintings invisible in this poem. But the pictures recognizably present in it are, in this order: *Summertime, Second Story Sunlight, Summer in the City, Self-Portrait* (1945), *Two Comedians, Jo Painting.*

"*The Drawer of Photographs.*" The lines in italics are taken from three late poems by Robert Lowell: "Half a Century Gone" (*Notebook*), "Purgatory" and "New York Again" (*The Dolphin*). It was Randall Jarrell who spoke of the "senseless originality" of Lowell's "thinginess."

"Continuing City." My title comes from Hebrews 13:14: "Here we have no continuing city, but we seek one to come." The Tranströmer line is important to me partly because of Robert Bly's commentary on it: " 'The children no one prays for' is a painful line. He is not coming down on the side of orthodox Christianity, and yet a part of him is aware that children are deprived, even endangered, by not being prayed for." In the Tenth Duino Elegy, Rilke invents new constellations for the Land of Pain, that the dead wander off into: *Die Sterne des Leidlands.* The reference to *Paradiso XXXIII* will probably be familiar to many readers.

"Recitation for the Dismantling of a Hydrogen Bomb." Any poem of this kind should, I think, be a collective as well as an individual undertaking. This one would not have taken the shape it did without the ABC-TV movie "The Day After"; Bach's St. Matthew Passion; Thomas J. J. Altizer and William Hamilton's *Radical Theology and the Death of God*; and Jonathan Schell's *The Fate of the Earth.* The work done in the Boston area in the late 1970s by Dr. Herbert Benson and Jonathan Kabat-Zinn on the use of meditation in the treatment of chronic pain offered a metaphor for what it could be like to survive, knowing that the means of collective self-destruction are always (conceptually) available.

A NOTE ON THE TYPE

This book was set on the linotype in Bodoni Book, named
after Giambattista Bodoni (1740–1813), son of a printer
of Piedmont. After gaining experience and fame as super-
intendent of the Press of the Propaganda in Rome, in 1768
Bodoni became the head of the ducal printing house at
Parma, which he soon made the foremost of its kind in
Europe. His *Manuale Tipografico*, completed by his widow
in 1818, contains 279 pages of type specimens, including
alphabets of about thirty languages. His editions of Greek,
Latin, Italian, and French classics are celebrated for their
typography. In type designing he was an innovator, making
his new faces rounder, wider, and lighter, with greater
openness and delicacy, and with sharper contrast between
the thick and thin lines.

Composed by Heritage Printers, Inc.
Charlotte, North Carolina
Printed and bound by Halliday Lithographers,
West Hanover, Massachusetts

Typography and binding
design by
Chip Kidd